SHAKEN

BY HIS PRESENCE

By Kim Wetteland

Pecan Grove Publishing
A division of Pecan Grove, LLC

Pecan Grove Publishing
www.pecangrovepublishing.com

Copyright © 2016, Kim Wetteland

All rights reserved, including the right to reproduce this book or portions thereof in any form whatsoever. All requests for reproduction must be made in writing to Pecan Grove Publishing, Rights Department, P.O. Box 5093, Woodridge, IL, 60517 or by email at permissions@pecangrovepublishing.com.

First edition, January, 2017

For information about bulk purchase and non-profit organization discounts, please contact Pecan Grove Publishing by email at npo@pecangrovepublishing.com, or visit our web site at www.pecangrovepublishing.com for more information.

Unless otherwise attributed, Scripture taken from the New King James Version®. Copyright © 1982 by Thomas Nelson. Used by permission. All rights reserved.

Cover design by Richard O. Ike.

Printed in the United States of America

10 9 8 7 6 5 4 3 2 1

ISBN 978-1-68128-003-5 (Print)
ISBN 978-1-68128-004-2 (Kindle)

Table of Contents

Introduction 1
Chapter One – Having a Blast with God! 3
Chapter Two – The Bus Stop 9
Chapter Three – Please Come See Me Again 15
Chapter Four – I'm Never Coming Back 21
Chapter Five – The Rain Began to Fall 27
Chapter Six – Deliverance Came Into the House 31
Chapter Seven – Pentecostal by the Book 37
Chapter Eight – A Visit from *the General* 43
Chapter Nine – Great Grace Came on All of Us 47
Chapter Ten – Placing the Shoe Where It Fits 53
Chapter Eleven – A Word of Exhortation for Church Members 61
Chapter Twelve – Developing a Culture of Corporate Prayer 65

Introduction

Prior to traveling full-time, for the past twenty-two years as a Missionary-Evangelist, I served thirteen years as the senior pastor of two local churches. For seven of those years I was the senior leader of Victory Christian Center in Des Moines, Iowa.

During my seven years at VCC, I had a deep passion to have our entire church family involved in corporate prayer. Although we offered several avenues of opportunity for our congregation to gather and pray throughout the week, only a very small number of people actually participated.

The only way that I was able to assemble all two-hundred members of our church family together to pray corporately, on a consistent basis, was by including ten minutes of corporate-congregational prayer into our main Sunday morning church services.

Our prayer meetings evolved into a living, breathing lifeline within the structure of our Sunday morning services, and became part of the culture of who we were as a church family.

None of us had a clue that establishing ten minutes of corporate-congregational prayer as a normal-regular part of our main Sunday morning services would result in the life changing, supernatural power of Jesus Christ moving in our midst in ways that we never could have planned for, dreamed of, or imagined.

I wrote this book to bless the body of Christ, and to help pastors and leaders experience the benefits of adopting a Book of Acts model of doing church, by including a slotted-time of corporate-congregational prayer into the main worship service.

The stories and real life testimonies you are about to read are all true. Corporate prayer in our main worship services united our entire church family together as a team. Truly, we were all – SHAKEN BY HIS PRESENCE!

Kim A. Wetteland
Missionary/Evangelist

Chapter One
Having a Blast with God!

Being a student in the theology department at Oral Roberts University was not easy. Each class was long, detailed, tedious, and carried the weight and expectation of achieving excellence.

One particular day was especially difficult. I had just finished a three hour examination in which the study of more than 400 pages of historical scholarship detailing the hypothetical existence of a Q Source as a possible explanation for the commonality of the three synoptic Gospels – Matthew, Mark, and Luke – were required. Mentally and physically, I was exhausted!

After consuming a typical "Jesus please help my dinner" in the school cafeteria, I headed straight to my dorm room, fell into bed, and collapsed. Following several hours of deep sleep the time was now 11 PM – my favorite hour of the day. Time to have a blast with Jesus.

Fun-Time with God!
I quickly changed clothes and ran out of my dorm room. Other students were finishing up their final studies for the day;

showering, brushing their teeth, and preparing to retire for the evening. Not me. I was so excited! I couldn't wait! This was my most-treasured time of the day!

I left EMR and began to walk across the beautiful university campus. While passing the Prayer Tower my eyes caught a glimpse of the illuminate stars in the Oklahoma sky. I lifted my hands with jubilation and began to praise and worship God in both English and other tongues as rivers of living water poured out of my spirit in a living relationship with the Creator of the universe. What a blast! This was my fun-time with God!

I sensed God's majestic, loving presence as my spirit intermingled with the Holy Spirit as other tongues of rivers of living water began to pour out of my spirit in a love relationship of communion with Jesus Christ. I could actually feel God with my spirit, hear Him personally call me by name, and speak to me.

> *My sheep hear My voice, and I know them, and they follow Me.*
>
> John 10:27

Why didn't anyone tell me that prayer was not just prayer? I mean the kind of prayer I was schooled in nearly killed those who participated; head-bowed, formal, lifeless, one-sided petitions that drained every ounce of energy from one's physical body and was so laborious and boring that people wanted to run from God instead of running to God.

After I received the baptism in the Holy Spirit prayer became life, enjoying God, talking with God, and actually hearing God talk back to me. No wonder Jesus described New Testament prayer as rivers of living, flowing, exciting, empowering, life producing water! Not only did I sense God with my spirit, I could feel His life, strength, and health coursing through my physical body (Romans 8:11).

> *He that believeth on me, as the scripture hath said, out of his belly shall flow rivers of living water. But this spake he of the Spirit, which they that believe on him should receive: for the Holy Ghost was not yet given; because that Jesus was not yet glorified.*
>
> John 7:38-39

I Could not Wait to Pray

After being baptized in the Holy Spirit, no one had to tell me to pray, convince me to pray, or force me to pray. I could not wait to pray! I did not want anything from God. I just wanted to know Him, to be with Him, to sense His presence and love for me, to hear His voice, to obey Him, and to discover His purpose and plan for my life. The One who hung on Calvary's cross and bled for me was no longer a distant-historical figure whom I did not know. Oh boy, did I know Him now! Jesus is not in the grave! He rose from the dead! He is alive! And I was actually talking with Him and was hearing Him talk back to me!

Every night, for several hours, I would walk the campus of Oral Roberts University worshiping God, praying in English, praying in other tongues, talking with God, hearing Him talk to me, singing in English, singing in other tongues, laughing, crying, and feeling His perfect love for me. This was not prayer as I was taught. This was life! This was a real relationship with Jesus!

This was fun and something I looked forward to with excitement!

I would ask Jesus questions about life, the Bible, and His will for my life. He would answer me, direct me to other Scripture, and freely share His wisdom and understanding (James 1:5). Jesus asked me questions too. I would search the Scriptures, listen to the Holy Spirit, and give Him my answers the following evening as we walked, talked, communed, and enjoyed one another's company again and again.

Grounded in God's Word

One night Jesus told me that He would never speak anything to me that did not line up with the Bible, and that if I ever heard a voice that spoke contrary to the Holy Scriptures, it was not Him speaking!

Sanctify them by Your truth. Your word is truth.

John 17:17

These lessons helped me understand that studying and being grounded in God's Word, the Bible, are vital, necessary keys for hearing and knowing the voice of our Savior. Those who try to hear God's voice without a solid foundation in God's Word end up hearing strange voices, believe goofy teachings, and fall into deception that brings hurt, pain, and confusion to marriages, homes, and families.

The more I studied the Holy Scriptures and walked the campus of Oral Roberts University every evening, talking to God, listening to Him, and at times crying as I felt His perfect love for me, the more I wanted to make surrendering my life to Jesus, something that I did daily, from my heart. I no longer wanted my will, my ways, and my plans. I wanted His will, His ways, and His plans for my life. I thoroughly enjoyed my routine-evening walk with Jesus and I was having a blast with God!

Chapter Two
The Bus Stop

Everything seemed to be completely normal. After my usual 11 PM walk with God, I returned to my dorm room, climbed into bed, but could not sleep. I tossed and turned until 2:30 AM. Finally, while praying softly under my breath, I said, "Lord, why can't I sleep?" To my complete shock, Jesus immediately responded to my question and replied, "Because I have an assignment for you. Get dressed immediately!"

I jumped out of bed and put on a pair of jeans and a T-shirt. My roommate, Don, recently surrendered his life to Jesus Christ, received the baptism in the Holy Spirit, and was full of enthusiasm. Don partied hard in his Grand Rapids, Michigan, high school. Involved in numerous fights, Don had one front tooth knocked out that was replaced with a gold tooth.

With his eyes barely open and the dorm room light flickering off of that gold tooth, Don asked, "What are you doing?" "The Lord told me to get dressed because He has an assignment for me," I replied. With a huge smile on his face, Don catapulted out of bed and said, "I wouldn't miss this for the world! I am going with you!"

Seeing in the Spirit

Upon leaving our dormitory, Don and I walked across the ORU campus departing the university grounds. Having no clue where we were going or what God had in mind, both of us were praying in other tongues. Every once in a while Don, who was a freshman, would say, "What's God saying to ya? What's God saying to ya?" He did this so frequently that I nearly wanted to slap him!

Suddenly, I saw a man standing under a streetlamp at a bus stop. I said, "Don, God wants us to speak with that man." Don replied, "What man?" "That man standing underneath the streetlamp at that bus stop 200 yards away," I responded. "Oh my gosh, you're seeing in the spirit," Don shouted with excitement!

As soon as Don spoke, I could no longer see the streetlamp, bus stop, or the man. I honestly wondered if I was imagining things. Don began to run in the general direction of the bus stop that neither of us could see. Having no clue if there really was a man standing at a bus stop, reluctantly, I began running after Don.

I've Been Waiting for You

After running for what seemed to be an eternity, a man dressed in an overcoat standing underneath a streetlamp at a bus stop finally came into view. Don and I paused a moment to catch our breath. We approached the man who turned slowly, looked directly into my eyes, pulled an 18-inch butcher knife out from underneath his overcoat, and said, "What took you so long? I've been waiting for you."

The Bus Stop

I was so startled that I nearly peed my pants! Did God send me out here in the middle of the night to be killed by a Jack the Ripper impersonator? With tear-filled eyes this young man, whose name was David, began to share his story.

David had just left the bedside of his younger brother Stephen, at St. Francis Hospital, who passed away from terminal brain cancer. "Stephen was a good boy," David said. "Why did he have to die? He kept telling me that he had perfect peace, not to worry about him, that he would be in heaven soon, and that I needed to surrender my life to Jesus Christ. And then while I was holding his hand, Stephen took his last breath and was gone."

I held David in my arms as he sobbed profusely. After drying his tears, David continued to detail the previous two hours. "I left St. Francis Hospital, went home and got this butcher knife, and have been wandering the streets of Tulsa. I've been telling God that if this Jesus whom my brother told me about, is really real, that He needed to get someone out of bed now and send them to me or I was going to kill myself with this butcher knife. What took you so long? I've been waiting for you," David cried with emotion.

I comforted David and shared my story with him of how I could not sleep and that Jesus told me to get out of bed, to get dressed, and to leave the university campus because He had something for me to do. After a few moments of solitude, I prayed with David to surrender his life to Jesus Christ. With a big grin on his face and the street lamp shimmering off of that gold front tooth, Don said with enthusiasm, "Now you need the Holy Ghost!"

"What is the Holy Ghost?" inquired David. "You're going to find out," exclaimed Don as he laughed like a little child!

Joy from the Holy Spirit

I asked Don to pray with David to receive the baptism in the Holy Spirit. Immediately, David began to speak in other tongues, laugh, cry, and praise God. "Jesus is so real," he shouted! David laughed and laughed and laughed as he prayed in tongues and kept saying, "I cannot believe this, my brother just died and I have such joy. Stephen was right. Jesus is so real!"

Do You Remember Me?

Several years had now passed. I graduated from ORU, met and married my wife Cherie in 1984, and completely forgot about leading David to Jesus at 2:30 AM.

Early one evening while dining with my new bride at a restaurant, a young man approached our table and said, "Do you remember me?" "No, sorry but I don't recall meeting you," I replied. "Well," the young man continued, "do you remember praying with a guy to surrender his life to Christ, at a bus stop at 2:30 AM, who was going to kill himself with a butcher knife because his brother just died at St. Francis Hospital?" Absolutely stunned, I said, "Yes, I remember." "I'm David, the guy you prayed with to receive Christ, and the baptism in the Holy Spirit, at that bus stop. I've been asking God to bring you across my path so I could thank you," he said.

David went on to tell Cherie and I that he had since attended Christ for the Nations in Dallas, Texas, just graduated from their Missions Program, was getting ready to leave the country for his first two-year furlough on the mission field in El Salvador, and wanted to thank me for obeying Jesus at 2:30 AM, getting out of bed, and leading him to Jesus Christ at that bus stop.

Prayer – A Normal Relationship

Needless to say, I was stunned. Vividly reflecting upon that evening, I had returned to my dorm room after several hours of walking and talking with Jesus, and was simply trying to go to sleep. The time was 2:30 AM. Jesus told me to get up, get dressed, and to leave my dorm room because He had an assignment for me. I obeyed Jesus' voice, left my dorm room in the middle of the night, and the rest is history. David, who was going to commit suicide, surrendered his life to Christ at a Tulsa bus stop, received the baptism in the Holy Spirit, graduated from the Missions Program at Christ for the Nations, and was now on the mission field in El Salvador.

Somehow, my prayer life had grown and developed into a close, conversational relationship with Jesus, that to me, seemed so normal. Truly, I was both, grateful and humbled by this experience.

Chapter Three
Please Come See Me Again

After receiving the baptism in the Holy Spirit, prayer was never an issue or something that I struggled to do consistently. Prayer became a real relationship, communing with God, enjoying His presence and company, talking with Him and hearing Him talk back to me. No one has ever had to force me, convince me, or give me some kind of daily-regimented plan in order to assist me in maintaining a regular prayer life. To me, prayer is not prayer as defined and understood by so many. Are you kidding? I get to spend time with God, talk to Him, and He talks back to me. Life just does not get any better than that! When my head lifts off the pillow each morning I can't wait to hear what God has to say to me!

> *My sheep hear My voice, and I know them, and they follow Me.*
>
> John 10:27

Just like in any relationship, though, I have discovered that if an individual can be trusted to be closed-mouthed and keep things private, God will open up to that person and share many things. God, however, does not have much to say to those who are known to gossip, sow discord, and blab everything they know. Even God has enough sense to remain silent and refrain from casting His pearls before swine, or people who cannot be trusted (Matthew 7:6).

Stop and Park Now!

After graduating from ORU, I worked for several years in the Tulsa area as a landscaper. After one particular long hard day, I was driving past Tulsa University and heard the crystal-clear voice of the Lord deep inside my spirit, "Stop your car and park now!"

Situations like this were becoming so normal. I did not even hesitate. I parked my car and began to walk across the TU campus. I had no idea where I was going or who the Lord wanted me to meet.

Suddenly, I had an urgency to enter the men's dormitory that housed international undergraduates from around the world. Students were everywhere. I easily passed by 50 to 70 young men but did not feel that I was to speak with anyone until I reached the third floor. Sitting alone at his desk was a Middle Eastern looking young man, named Mohamed, who motioned me to enter his room. I complied with his request and began to tell him about the good news of Jesus Christ.

Mohamed spoke fluent Aramaic but not much English. Sharing the gospel with him proved to be very difficult. Mohamed kept saying, "Jesus good man, a prophet, but is not God. Allah is God."

Please Come See Me Again

After about 10 minutes of making no headway, I started to leave and Jesus spoke something in my spirit that stunned me. He said, "Don't leave! Talk to him in other tongues!" I said, "Lord, he will think I am goofy if I talk to him in other tongues." "He already thinks you are goofy," the Lord replied. "Talk to him in other tongues!"

I headed back into the room, looked directly into Mohamed's eyes, and began speaking to him in other tongues. I could sense the Holy Spirit leading me as various tonal pitches and points of emphasis were placed on different syllables of sound coming from my mouth. Mohamed's ears perked up and his eyes seemed to enlighten as if he understood everything I was saying.

When I finished, Mohamed grabbed me by the shoulders, kissed me on the left side of my cheek and then on the right side, and said, "You are a good man. Please, come back and see me after many days."

Aramaic New Testament
After returning home, I showered, ate dinner, and called my good friend Samir who was a student in the Graduate School of Business at ORU. Samir grew up in the Middle East and spoke fluent Aramaic. After hearing my story, Samir suggested that I order a New Testament in Aramaic from a local Christian bookstore. When the New Testament arrives, together, we would visit Mohamed and give him the Aramaic New Testament.

The New Testament Arrived
Three weeks later, I received a call from the Christian Book Store informing me that the Aramaic New Testament had

arrived. I called Samir, we picked up the New Testament from the Book Store, and headed for Tulsa University to visit Mohamed.

Upon arriving at TU we parked our car, quickly walked to the International Dorm, climbed the stairs to the third floor, made our way towards the end of the hallway, and there, sitting at his desk, was Mohamed.

After greeting one another and introducing my friend, Samir and Mohamed began speaking to each other in Aramaic. Both men were motioning with their hands and conversed for quite some time. Finally, with bowed heads, Samir and Mohamed joined hands and prayed. Samir gave Mohamed the Aramaic New Testament, we said our goodbyes, and departed as Mohamed sat at his desk reading the gospel of John.

Give Me Something to Eat

When we got back to our car Samir said, "Kim, you will never believe what happened! When you began speaking to Mohamed in other tongues, you actually spoke to him in fluent Aramaic about his younger sister who was on her death bed in Lebanon. Mohamed was awaiting a call from his father to let him know that his sister had died. You told him that Jesus was healing his sister as a sign to their entire family that He was God, the Messiah, and their Savior. When you left, Mohamed called his father in Lebanon. When the phone rang, his sister woke from her coma, sat straight up in bed, and said, 'give me something to eat I am hungry.'"

Mohamed and his entire family surrendered their lives to Christ as a result of this miraculous visitation from Jesus. Due to

Please Come See Me Again

persecution, they left Lebanon and currently reside in the United States.

Chapter Four
I'm Never Coming Back

Talking with God and hearing Him talk back to me became a normal-daily part of my relationship with Jesus Christ. My prayer life was never forced. Instead, prayer for me became as natural as sitting down with a close friend and conversing over coffee. As a young pastor, I instinctively knew that a similar type of natural, unhindered corporate-congregational prayer, in our local churches, was vital. Peter was released from prison when an entire local church family prayed for his deliverance, continuously, without ceasing.

> *Peter was therefore kept in prison, but constant prayer was offered to God for him by the church.*
>
> Acts 12:5

The supernatural power of God seems to have a direct correlation to every member of a local church assembly all praying together, corporately, at the same time. For the Early Church this type of community prayer was as natural as breathing.

Monday evening was the time we set aside for our church family to come together in united prayer for one hour. And yet, in a congregation of two-hundred people, only ten to fifteen members usually participated. This really bothered me. With varied work schedules, school, homework, and other responsibilities; assembling the entire church family together in one place to pray, all at the same time, seemed impossible. What was I to do?

Cancel Monday Evening Prayer

God's direction became crystal clear – cancel intercessory prayer on Monday evening and bring the prayer meeting into the main Sunday morning service.

The whole idea of including an extended time of intercessory prayer as an integral part of our main Sunday morning service was revolutionary. I was not aware of any pastors, or local churches, doing this. And yet, the more I thought about bringing the prayer meeting into our main Sunday morning service, the more it made sense. The entire Pentecostal movement was birthed because the Early Church had extended times of prayer in their main worship services.

> *These all continued with one accord in prayer and supplication...*
>
> Acts 1:14

And after all, Jesus said, "...It is written, My house shall be called a house of prayer" (Matthew 21:13). I knew why prayer was no longer a part of our American public schools. This happened as a result of a decision made by the United States Supreme Court. But how have regular-extended times of prayer completely disappeared from the main Sunday morning services in 99% of our Evangelical and Pentecostal churches in America?

Time to Prepare

Our plan was to cancel Monday evening prayer and to incorporate ten minutes of structured, yet unhindered, intercessory prayer into our main Sunday morning worship services. Making this change would allow us to have all two-hundred members of our church family praying together corporately, for ten minutes every week, instead of having just a handful of people praying for an hour on Monday evening.

For three months I taught and thoroughly instructed our church family about the importance and benefits of corporate-congregational prayer and shared the vision of making ten minutes of prayer a normal-vital part of our main Sunday worship service. During this time, I met weekly to pray with fifteen men whom I trained to lead prayer in our services. Praying with these men regularly was a necessary part of a hands-on training process to ensure that each man became comfortable and fluent, to boldly pray in English and in other tongues, publicly.

I Was Shocked!

The big day arrived. Our first Sunday morning service with ten minutes of full-blown, Book-of-Acts-type intercessory prayer was here. Everything was flawless. The men assigned to lead prayer did a tremendous job and the congregation followed suit with strong, intense, unified intercession. I was ecstatic! I finally discovered and implemented a feasible way for all 200 of our church members to pray together corporately, on a consistent basis – by bringing the prayer meeting into our main Sunday morning worship service!

At the end of the service I rushed to the foyer with excitement to love on our church family while they departed the building. The first gentlemen I greeted said, "Well, I'll tell you what, Pastor. If this is going to be a church that prays like this every Sunday, then I am never coming back!"

Needless to say, I was completely stunned. If only one individual would have felt this way, that would have been one thing, but 30 members of our church family left that day and never returned because we decided to step outside the box of, *church-as-usual Americanized Christianity,* and made ten minutes of Holy Ghost prayer a vital part of our main Sunday morning worship service. A price would have to be paid to have a genuine, Book-of-Acts-type, Pentecostal Church.

The Holy Spirit's Work of Grace
Now He who searches the hearts knows what the mind of the Spirit is, because He makes intercession for the saints according to the will of God.

Romans 8:27

I sought God for an answer regarding why people would leave our church because we made a change to include ten minutes of prayer into our main Sunday morning worship services. Two things were revealed to me.

First, during times of corporate-congregational prayer, the Holy Spirit searches the hearts of all, revealing and exposing weaknesses, shortcomings, and hidden sins. Some have not been equipped to cooperate with this level of personal sanctification due to popular teachings claiming that only good, happy, elated, and wonderful feelings of joy are experienced when the Holy Spirit shows up. This could not be further from the truth!

I spent the next eight weeks teaching our church family about the foundational practicalities of the Holy Spirit's work of sanctification that would be applied to our lives as we prayed together corporately. Methodically, I instructed how that by grace, our hearts would be searched during corporate-congregational prayer, and that weaknesses, shortcomings, and sins would be revealed to each of us personally, so we may cooperate with the Holy Spirit's searching-work of grace by choosing to take a posture of submission and asking Christ to cleanse our lives by the Holy Spirit's merciful work of sanctification.

There Are Some Who Oppose Everything
Secondly, some people are simply resistant and are opposed to any expression of prayer that crosses the line of our self-imposed, heads bowed, eyes closed, we-must-pray-quietly, religious boundaries. This type of individual, of whom some are Pentecostal pastors, are simply intolerant of any type of loud prayer in other tongues, accompanied by intercessory groanings in the spirit.

Eventually, the 30 individuals who chose to leave were replaced by others and our entire church family grew to understand how that, by grace, the Holy Spirit deeply searches our hearts during corporate prayer, and purges our lives from dirt, crud, and evil influences; so we may surrender to Christ's sanctifying grace, and live in real victory over sin and dysfunctional behavior.

Corporate-congregational prayer and worship eventually became the culture, lifeline, and life blood of our entire church family in a way that none of us ever could have expected or imagined.

Chapter Five
The Rain Began to Fall

After several months of including ten minutes of intercessory prayer in our main Sunday morning worship services, corporate-congregational prayer became a normal, cultural part of who we were in Christ as a local church family.

Praise and worship acquired a new dynamic and matured from just songs that we were singing, to strong, exuberant, spontaneous praise and worship that was filled with God's presence, power, and majesty. Our worship team began to lead the congregation in Holy Spirit inspired songs of surrendered-worship to the King. These new songs that none of us had previously heard or ever sung, were given to our music team as gifts from the Holy Spirit that became a commonly recognized trait of our Sunday morning worship services in our community. In fact, spontaneous, Holy Spirit inspired songs became so commonplace, that this type of worship became part of our culture as a local church family. We incorporated these new songs into praise and worship for all of our services, conferences, and special events.

Everyone, including visiting pastors, worship leaders, and other congregants wanted to know where we acquired our music. We would laugh with joy, and say, "...the Holy Spirit began giving us these worship songs when we instituted ten minutes of corporate prayer into our Sunday morning services."

I never realized how far below our potential in Christ we were living and functioning as a church family until nine months after we made ten minutes of corporate-congregational prayer a normal part of our main Sunday morning services.

Where Did All These People Come From?
On one particular Sunday 40 visitors showed up out of nowhere. And, believe me, when your average Sunday morning attendance comprises a membership of 200, everyone notices when an additional 40 people arrive.

After the service was over my wife and I met with all of our special guests in the hospitality room. Many were visiting relatives, some were just passing through, and others were in town on business. We had a wonderful time.

Just as my wife and I were getting ready to walk out the door, my head usher stopped me and said, "Pastor, you have to come in the administration office immediately!" When I inquired about the reason for this, he just said, "Please, just come right away!"

Upon entering the office I noticed all of the visitor cards from that day, 40 of them, were laying on the desk. "Pastor, you'll never believe this in your life! You have got to read these visitor cards," my head usher exclaimed!

As I read the section on each card detailing how each visitor came to our morning worship service, needless to say, I could hardly believe what I was reading. Almost every visitor card reiterated something that went like this, "We were driving down the street minding our own business, got caught up in the traffic flow, ended up in your parking lot, and the attendant directed us into a parking space. Since we were already parked, we decided to come inside and find out what was going on."

Is This Really Happening?

Visitor card after visitor card conveyed the same, basic rationale for attending our Sunday morning worship service. And, the thing that was even harder to comprehend was that this phenomenon continued to happen every Sunday for the next four consecutive weeks. And, during this four week time frame, 185 people were baptized in the Holy Spirit with the evidence of speaking in other tongues!

We had no idea that including ten minutes of corporate-congregational prayer into our main Sunday morning worship services would produce such life changing manifestations of God's presence and supernatural power. None of us knew what was going to happen from Sunday to Sunday. The rain of God's presence began to fall in our midst. Literally, we all felt like we were living in The Book of Acts!

Chapter Six
Deliverance Came Into the House

Larry was one of the kindest individuals I have ever had the privilege to know as a friend. He was like a son to me and everyone in our church family loved Larry. He was, and still is, a fantastic human being.

Pastor, I'm a Homosexual

I will never forget the day Larry told me that he was a homosexual. Did we reject Larry? Ostracize him? Cast him aside and turn our backs on him? On the contrary, our entire church family rallied around Larry with grace and truth because we loved him.

> *You shall not lie with a male as with a woman. It is an abomination*
>
> Leviticus 18:22

As Christians we cannot accept and condone any lifestyle choice that God says is immoral, wrong, and sinful. And yet, with a recent Supreme Court decision making same-sex marriage legal in America, pastors, leaders, and Christians have come under intense pressure to accept homosexuality, lesbianism, gender identity choice, and same-sex marriage as normal-alternative lifestyles. Those who voice opposing views to the new political, social, and societal norms are labeled as bigots, homophobic, are stripped of their free-speech rights under the guise of hate speech, and are being charged with discrimination and hate crimes.

Listen, it is still possible to hate sin but love the sinner! We hated the sin of homosexuality but we dearly loved Larry and offered him the same grace in Christ we would lovingly share with anyone who strays from God's will concerning purity in sexual relationships.

I Feel Like God Made Me This Way
I am not sure how many times that I read Scripture verses to Larry, counseled him, anointed him with oil, and earnestly prayed for him to be set free. Nothing I did, however, seemed to have any effect.

During one of our final counseling sessions, Larry looked me straight in the eye and said, "Pastor, I know what I am going to say is not true according to what the Bible teaches, but I just feel that God made me to be this way."

The Deliverer Showed Up
Several weeks had passed since my counseling session with Larry. Sunday morning had arrived and it had now been about one year since we incorporated ten minutes of congregational prayer into our main worship services.

On this particular Sunday, prayer was unusually strong, bold, and militant. Our church family was very comfortable with all types of prayers, petitions, and the groanings of Spirit-inspired intercession that included loud-bold prayer in both English and other tongues. This Sunday, however, something was different.

Suddenly, our worship team began to sing a brand new Holy Spirit inspired song. "The Deliverer is coming! The Deliverer is coming! The Deliverer from Zion is coming, and His Name is Jesus!"

The entire congregation chimed in with exuberant worship and uplifted hands. Then, the song shifted to the present tense. "The Deliverer is here! The Deliverer is here! The Deliverer from Zion is here, and His Name is Jesus!"

The sanctuary literally exploded with loud, strong, authoritative-prophetic praise! "The Deliverer is here! The Deliverer is here! The Deliverer from Zion is here, and His Name is Jesus!" The whole congregation sang!

While the church continued singing this song from the Spirit, Larry slipped out from his chair, ran to the front of the sanctuary and collapsed at the altar. The congregation shifted out of praise and back into strong, intercessory prayer in other tongues as a team of altar workers surrounded Larry, laid hands upon him, and began to pray. Everyone, from the altar workers to each member of the congregation was very well trained and knew how to function together as a team.

Then, my head usher who also was praying for Larry, approached me and said, "Pastor, the Lord has given me a word of knowledge for Larry."

Let two or three prophets speak, and let the others judge.

1 Corinthians 14:29

My men knew the importance of following proper governmental protocol for sharing a prophetic utterance. So, my head usher whispered the word of knowledge in my ear so it could be appropriately judged. I immediately responded, "Go whisper this in Larry's ear but don't allow it to go over the microphone."

My head usher knelt beside Larry and whispered the following word of knowledge in his ear. "Larry, when you were a child a man raped you. When this terrible violation occurred, a soul tie was created inside of you with males, and caused you to have sexual desires for other men. From that moment you began to think that God made you this way. But today, the Deliverer from Zion is here and He is completely setting you free!" I was told that Larry's blood curdling scream could be all the way downstairs in the nursery.

The Wedding
A year later I heard rumors that Larry and a young woman by the name of Brenda were dating. Shortly thereafter, Larry called and asked if I would meet with them. Several months later I had the honor of joining this young couple in marriage. They had several beautiful children and became the best Children's Pastors I ever had!

Corporate Prayer Changed Everything
I'm convinced that this miracle of deliverance, amongst other real-life testimonies in this book, never would have happened if ten minutes of corporate-congregation prayer had not been

included as a normal part of our main Sunday morning worship services.

This, of course, went completely against the grain of what every other Pentecostal Church in our city was doing. But, I can mark the day that God began to visit our local church assembly. It was the day we cancelled Monday evening prayer and decided to bring the prayer meeting into our main Sunday morning worship services.

Chapter Seven
Pentecostal by the Book

The Pentecostal experience involves far more than being baptized in the Holy Spirit with the evidence of speaking in other tongues, accompanied by the activity of the gifts of the Spirit in our local church services (1 Cor. 12:4-11).

For the Early Church, Pentecost was birthed, rooted, and grounded in an entire culture of corporate prayer that functioned as a normal part of their main worship services. In fact, it could be argued that a local church is not truly Pentecostal unless times of corporate-congregational prayer are a living-functional part of that church's primary worship services.

In Acts Chapter Two, a specific, historical milestone took place on the day of Pentecost and is recorded in Scripture. This initial outpouring of the Holy Spirit was accompanied by the evidence of speaking in other tongues. Alone, by itself, this event does not provide us with a complete picture of Pentecost. When Acts Chapter Two is combined with Acts Chapter Four, however, we are given a much broader photograph of how a true Pentecostal Church is capable of functioning.

31 And when they had prayed, the place where they were assembled together was shaken; and they were all filled with the Holy Spirit, and they spoke the word of God with boldness.

32 Now the multitude of those who believed were of one heart and one soul; neither did anyone say that any of the things he possessed was his own, but they had all things in common.

33 And with great power the apostles gave witness to the resurrection of the Lord Jesus. And great grace was upon them all.

34 Nor was there anyone among them who lacked...

Acts 4:31-34

Corporate Prayer Was a Vital-Living Part of the Early Church's Main Worship Services

And when they prayed, the place where they were assembled together was shaken...

Acts 4:31

The key word in this verse is *assembled* (Gr: *sunago* – to collect, convene, gather, assemble, or come together). Clearly, this is a picture of the main worship service in the Early Church – a Pentecostal Church. And what were they doing? All 5,000 of the men, plus the women and children, were all praying together corporately in their main worship service! Corporate-congregational prayer was a principal foundation that served a living-functional role in their primary, worship services that formed the identity of the Early Church as being distinctly Pentecostal!

Fueled by this critical foundation of corporate-congregational prayer in their main worship services, seven key elements became a normal-cultural part of the Book of Acts Church.

1. God's Presence and Power Were Present
God's presence, and His power, were present in the main worship services of the Early Church. As they prayed corporately, "...the place where they were assembled together was shaken" (Acts 4:31) with the supernatural, life-changing power of Jesus Christ.

2. All Were Filled with the Holy Spirit
In the Early Church, Holy Spirit baptisms occurred as a natural byproduct of corporate-congregation prayer being an inclusive part of their primary worship services. "And when they had prayed the place where they were assembled together was shaken; **and they were all filled with the Holy Spirit**" (Acts 4:31).

3. Spoke God's Word Boldly
The apostles, prophets, evangelists, pastors, and teachers were not the only ones who spoke God's word with boldness. All 5,000 men, plus the women and children, communicated their faith in Christ with clarity.

4. Every Church Member Was Committed to the Vision
The entire church family "...were of one heart and one soul" (Acts 4:32). Every church member was fully-committed to the vision of Jesus Christ as a team-member that served. Considering that 9% of Christians link to Christ's vision and serve in the average Evangelical or Pentecostal church in

America, this may be the single-most amazing byproduct of having corporate-congregational prayer as a normal part of the main Sunday morning worship services. Amazing! Every church member was planted in their local church, linked to the vision, and served in some capacity of in-house or outreach ministry.

5. The Apostles Ministered with Great Power

Many have been under the impression that the Early Church apostles functioned in great power simply because, they were apostles. I do not believe this is the case. Look at the Scriptural context! "And with great power the apostles gave witness to the resurrection of the Lord Jesus" (Acts 4:33). Why? This occurred because 100% of the Early Church family prayed together corporately in all of their main worship services!

The power that the apostles walked in had nothing to do with them, solely, as individuals. This was a team effort. They all prayed together corporately, thus, the apostles were able to give witness to the resurrection of Christ with great power. This was a genuine, Biblical, New Testament, Pentecostal Church!

6. Great Grace Rested on Everyone

The Greek word for grace is *Charis*, which signifies graciousness, liberality, benefit, and divine favor. Great grace (not just grace) did not just come on a few church members, but upon everyone because corporate prayer was a regular part of their primary worship services!

7. No One Lacked Financially
In this particular Early Church there were 5,000 men plus the women and children. Not even one of them lacked financially.

In one of the churches where I served as senior pastor, we too, experienced the miraculous phenomenon of having every church member gainfully employed without anyone lacking financially. This happened after we included ten minutes of corporate-congregational prayer into our main Sunday morning worship services. Great grace visited all of us, and not even one of our church members lacked financially!

We Are Living Far Below Our Potential
What would happen if we decided to truly become Pentecostal, like the Book of Acts Church, and include corporate-congregational prayer in our main Sunday morning worship services?

Well, let's just say that many of us would discover that we have been living way below our potential in Christ as a local church family. Corporate prayer as a vital part of our primary Sunday morning worship services is a key distinctive of being a Pentecostal Church. It's what I call being Pentecostal by the book!

Chapter Eight
A Visit from *the General*

Being the senior pastor of a local church that included ten minutes of corporate-congregational prayer in the main Sunday morning worship service required constant training, instruction, examination, monitoring, and preparation.

Every week we knew that corporate prayer would take place for at least ten minutes (sometimes longer), followed by praise and worship, announcements, tithes and offerings, a message from God's Word, and an altar call with specific ministry.

But, from Sunday to Sunday there was an element of the unknown that always would occur in every one of our main services. How does one prepare an entire staff, ushers, greeters, parking lot attendants, altar workers, children's ministry and nursery workers, and security for something that is going to happen, but you have no clue what it will be until it happens?

Such was the case during one of the numerous visits made to our local church by the late, great Missionary-Evangelist and Pastor, Dr. Lester Sumrall, also known as *The General*.

The General is Here
Every time Dr. Lester Sumrall visited us, it seemed as if the entire city showed up. We always ended up turning away hundreds of people.

As the service began, Dr. Sumrall and our regular church congregation were very comfortable with our usual ten minutes of corporate-congregational prayer. Many visitors, however, including other Pentecostal and spirit-filled pastors, just stood there and seemed to not even have a clue what was going on.

The prayer time was unusually strong, loud-bold intercession in other tongues, almost with a militant flavor. The atmosphere was quite tense and it was obvious that, even by our standards, this was not going to be a normal service!

The Glory Fell
While transitioning into worship from prayer, a sudden and unexpected shift occurred as our praise and worship team began to play and sing a glorious song of surrendering and bowing to Christ. This song was given to them by the Holy Spirit, they ran with it, our tech-team quickly got the words on the big screen, the entire congregation joined in with many kneeling at the altar and bowing from ones heart to the King of Kings. This was the only song we sang and no one outside our own church family knew that this was a new song given to us, instantaneously, as a gift from the Holy Spirit.

Waves of God's presence and glory crescendoed through the sanctuary for 30 minutes. When Dr. Sumrall stepped to the pulpit, believers were still on their knees worshipping Christ. No one wanted this refreshing time in the presence of God to end.

A Visit from the General

Pastor, the Fire Department is Here
Shortly after Dr. Sumrall began to preach, my head usher tapped me on my shoulder and said, "Pastor, the fire department is in our foyer. They have received numerous calls from people claiming that flames of fire are shooting out from the roof of our building." "Is our building on fire? Did you check?" I inquired. "Yes, Pastor", my usher replied, "we thoroughly inspected the building and there is no fire. But the Fire Marshal insists on inspecting the attic to make sure there is no fire."

Unfortunately, we were meeting in an old building and the only entrance to the attic was a small door in the ceiling, directly above the pulpit where Dr. Sumrall was preaching.

Without any announcement or warning, five firefighters in full-gear, began marching down the center isle towards Dr. Lester Sumrall. "What's going on here, Pastor? Why are these firemen walking down the aisle while I'm preaching? Don't you have your church in order?" exclaimed the General!

I tried to explain the situation to Dr. Sumrall regarding the numerous phone calls reporting that flames of fire were shooting from the top of the roof and that the firemen wanted to inspect the attic. Upon finding out that the only entrance to the attic was the small door, directly over the platform and above his head, in the ceiling, Dr. Sumrall looked at the firemen and, with authority said, "Haven't you ever heard of the manifestation of the Holy Spirit in flaming tongues of fire? No one is going in that attic. Now sit down and listen to the Holy Word of God!"

My ushers grabbed five-folding chairs, placed them in the center aisle, and to my utter astonishment, the firemen disregarded the fire code, sat in those chairs dressed in full-gear, and listened to Dr. Lester Sumrall teach the Word of God.

A Powerful Move of the Spirit
At the conclusion of Dr. Sumrall's message, the Holy Spirit moved powerfully. Nearly everyone in that sanctuary dropped to their knees or fell to the floor weeping. Only the five firemen and Dr. Sumrall were left standing. And, with great honor and compassion, Dr. Sumrall personally prayed with each fireman to receive the baptism in the Holy Spirit.

A Supernatural Offering to Feed the Poor
An offering was received for Dr. Lester Sumrall's *End-Time Joseph Feed the Hungry Program*. In my life, I have never witnessed such an offering. Four-hundred people filled our sanctuary, many of whom were teens, young dads and moms, elderly, and very average people. The amount of the offering received that evening to feed the poor was $19,300.

Truly, when all of us prayed together corporately that evening, *the place where we assembled together was shaken with the supernatural, life-changing power of Jesus Christ* (Acts 4:31). All of us were humbled to be a part of such a historic service and to be present to hear one of Dr. Lester Sumrall's final sermons before he went to heaven. What an honor to have had *A Visit from the General.*

Chapter Nine
Great Grace Came on All of Us

I'll never forget the day Becky walked into one our church services, surrendered her life to Christ, and received the baptism in the Holy Spirit with the immediate evidence of speaking in other tongues. She was gleaming from ear to ear!

Several weeks later Becky approached me after one of our services with questions about tithing. "Pastor," Becky inquired, "I hear you talk about giving our tithes all the time. I'm not married now, but when I was married my husband never even owned a tie!" "Not ties, Becky! Tithes," I said with laughter.

I explained that tithes are 10% of our gross income, which belongs to the Lord, and that giving God that portion of our income, which belongs to Him, is our response of honor and obedience, which is called *tithing*.

Without any warning, these big crocodile tears began to run down Becky's cheeks. "What's wrong, Becky?", I inquired. Becky explained that she was unemployed with no source of income to be able to honor God with His tithe. Suddenly, a huge smile appeared on Becky's face. "Pastor, would it be possible for me to tithe my time until I find a job?" she asked with excitement!

Serving, a Key to Greatness

Becky worked harder and served with more joy than anyone I knew. No one at Victory Christian Center was allowed to volunteer! Let me explain.

I methodically instructed our entire church family that, according to the teachings of Jesus we are all servants (not volunteers), and that all of us are required to serve in some aspect of in-house or outreach-type of ministry. So, at Victory Christian Center, we never referred to anyone as a volunteer – we were all servants!

> *But he who is greatest among you shall be your servant.*
>
> Matthew 23:11

Of all the illustrations that could have been used in discussing the various paths that lead an individual to a life of lasting value, excellence, and quality, Jesus confirmed that true greatness grows and matures in the lives of those who serve.

During my 13 years as a senior pastor I was frequently known to say, *"If I cannot get you to serve then I cannot help your life."* In fact, my congregation heard me repeat this with such regularity that I would voice the first half of this sentence, "If I cannot get you to serve...", and they would all chime in together and finish the thought, by saying,*"...then you cannot help our lives, Pastor."*

I was blessed to be the pastor of a church where all 200 of our congregants willingly chose to serve in some type of capacity. *A serving church is a powerful church* was another one of my frequently, verbalized truisms.

Not even once, did I ever ask for volunteers, or publicly say that volunteers were needed. Why? Because volunteering is merely a task that anyone may choose to accept or decline. Serving, however, is part of who we are in Christ. So, I thoroughly taught serving to our church family as one of the vital, in Christ realities. *Thus, serving became a natural expression of who we were in Christ, individuality and corporately, and became part of the culture of who we were as a church family!* The result – everyone began to serve!

Trust God for Favor

After receiving her GED, Becky began to submit applications for employment with no success. Then one Sunday, during my sermon, I casually mentioned that those who needed employment should apply for jobs that will compensate them at the income level needed to sufficiently provide for the needs of their family, even if they are not qualified to do that particular job. "Trust God to give you favor so the employer will hire and train you to do the job that you are not qualified to do," were the instructions I gave to my congregation.

She Landed the Job!

Becky arrived at church with excitement and was beaming from ear to ear! "Pastor, I did exactly what you taught us to do. I applied for a job that I am not qualified for, but the salary is at the income level that I need to provide for my family," Becky exclaimed with elation!

Becky's name, and need for favor, was projected onto the big screen in our sanctuary during corporate prayer in that Sunday morning service. Our entire church family surrounded Becky with an overwhelming display of encouragement, support, and faith-filled prayers. Prayer for Becky continued nearly 20 minutes, followed by lots of hugs, tears, and reassurance. Everyone deeply loved Becky.

The following Sunday, Becky stood before our entire congregation and shared a testimony of how God gave her favor during the job interview. The employer hired Becky and agreed to train her for a position for which she had no qualifications. Our entire church family celebrated with shouts of joy that transitioned right into our normal ten minutes of corporate-congregational prayer that flowed right into a powerful time of Spirit-led praise and worship.

For our local church, this type of structure became normal. And, for all of us, prayer was no longer prayer in a traditional, regimented sense. Prayer became life, relationship, and the way we breathed!

No One Lacked Financially

Becky was not the only member of or church family who landed a great job. From the day we made corporate-congregational prayer part of our main Sunday morning services, life improved for everyone in our congregation!

> "...And great grace was upon them all. Nor was there anyone among them who lacked;"
>
> Acts 4:33-34

Not even one of us lacked financially. Things were not always this way. Initially, many struggled and some were on public assistance. But the day we cancelled Monday evening prayer and brought the prayer meeting into our Sunday morning service, everything changed! Great grace came on all of us, and not even one member of our church family lacked financially. No one had any regrets about the decision we made to include ten minutes of corporate-congregational prayer into our primary Sunday morning worship services.

Chapter Ten
Placing the Shoe Where It Fits

Although there are some pockets of exception to this fact, the average local church in America has absolutely no times of corporate-congregational prayer included as a normal, regular part of their main worship services.

We talk about prayer, teach and preach about prayer, have prayer seminars, hold prayer summits, drink coffee and eat donuts for 55 minutes of our 1 hour pastors prayer meetings, and once a year we remind ourselves of the need to implement 2 Chronicles 7:14. But when it comes right down to the nitty-gritty of actually praying corporately in our main worship services, we simply don't do it!

The Cry for National Revival
Throughout our nation I hear the same comments, everywhere, from those who are pastors and leaders in the body of Christ, "We desperately need a move of God in America! Revival is imperative! Our churches must have a fresh outpouring of the Holy Spirit!"

So, while we sit around drinking coffee, pontificating, and discussing the theological ramifications regarding our need for revival, as we pretentiously boast those *come to Jesus looks on our faces,* have we ever, even once, thought about Christ's, desperate need for pastors and leaders who will allow times of corporate-congregational prayer to be included back into our main worship services so we actually can have a move of God in America?

The Hard Facts

Let's face the facts! In our typical American church we have twenty to thirty minutes slotted for praise and worship, five to seven minutes for a special song or a performance from the choir, three minutes for high-tech video announcements, one or two minutes to remember the sick in prayer, five minutes to receive tithes and offerings, twenty to forty minutes for the preaching and teaching of God's Word, and thirty seconds to five minutes for an altar call or a closing doxology.

But, where are the scheduled slots of time in our services, for our entire church families to intercede, cry out to God, and pray together corporately as a congregation?

Again, other than a few pockets that are an exception to this rule, this type of corporate-congregational prayer simply does not exist in our American churches! From our famous TV preachers of the mega churches to our unknown pastors in small, rural communities, we are all so busy doing *church as usual,* that we simply don't talk to God anymore.

Nothing is Ever Done
From the time I've been a teenager I have heard the same "If My people who are called by My name..." rhetoric, spouted every year, for 45 straight years.

We talk about 2 Chronicles 7:14, write books on the subject, and use gimmicks in an attempt to generate excitement. But nothing that would dare challenge or shake the *status quo;* or require any major change, or adjustment in the way we orchestrate our worship services, is ever done that will allow us to accommodate God and obey Him.

Nothing that I Tried Worked
Prior to traveling full-time as a missionary evangelist, I served as the senior pastor of Victory Christian Center in Des Moines, Iowa. The responsibility of providing instruction, and opportunities, for every member of our church family to participate in some facet of corporate prayer rested squarely upon my shoulders as the senior leader, in charge.

I tried several, various avenues of implementation in order to include prayer into the culture of who we were as a local church family: Monday evening prayer, men's prayer breakfasts, women's prayer retreats, youth prayer advances, and pre-service prayer, were among the many opportunities we provided to make prayer available for all.

No matter what opportunities were used as a vehicle to make times of corporate prayer available to our congregation, only a fraction of our entire church family actually were able to participate. Nothing that I tried to consistently gather all 200 members of our church family together (at the same time) for corporate prayer, worked.

The Business Model
If a business owner managed a company of 100 employees, but used an operating system that only allowed for 15 of those individuals to actually work (even though all 100 employees were paid a full wage), would this make sense? Of course not!

And yet, this is exactly what I was doing with the manner in which I was implementing corporate prayer. Two-hundred people comprised the congregants of Victory Christian Center and I was the senior pastor of every one of these precious individuals. But, the avenues that I was utilizing to provide venues of corporate prayer only offered a realistic opportunity for a very small portion of our church family to be able to participate.

I Was Only Pastoring Part of God's Flock
"...take care of the group of people you are responsible for. They are God's flock"

1 Peter 5:2 ERV

I was responsible to shepherd and guide God's entire flock, not just part of it. Every member of our congregation sat under my teaching ministry and received instruction, but only 10% came out for prayer on an off night, or arrived early to be a part of pre-service prayer.

How could I, as the senior pastor, adequately guard and protect our entire church family if I was only leading a very small segment of our members to a foundational, New Testament place of relational-security with God? This place of safety (corporate-congregational prayer) is for every member of Christ's body, not just a small segment of the church family!

I was providing several avenues for prayer and expecting all the church members to participate. As a pastor, I was forgetting that the people whom I was responsible to guard, guide, and protect, were all at different stages of growth and maturity. Some were brand-new babies in Christ and incapable of comprehending the importance of consistently praying together, corporately, with the entire church family.

> *Obey those who rule over you, and be submissive, for they watch out for your souls, as those who must give account...*
>
> Hebrews 13:17

The shoe of responsibility (to make sure that every member of Christ's body were involved in corporate prayer) was being placed exactly where it is supposed to fit – upon me as the pastor. I was the one, who was accountable to God, to do something about this.

Christ's Vision Regarding Corporate Prayer

I really had no legitimate excuse. We already had a time where every member of our church family showed up and assembled together weekly – our main Sunday morning worship service.

While quoting Isaiah 56:7, Jesus distinctly understood corporate-congregational prayer as something to be enjoyed as a normal-relational part of our primary worship services, saying, "It is written, My house shall be called a house of prayer..." (Matthew 21:13).

> *Even them I will bring to My holy mountain, And make them joyful in My house of prayer. Their burnt offerings and their sacrifices Will be accepted on My altar; For My house shall be called a house of prayer for all nations."*
>
> Isaiah 56:7

The Hebrew word used for prayer, twice in Isaiah 56:7, is *tphillah;* which means *house of intercession!* Clearly, Jesus envisioned corporate-congregational intercessory prayer as a common-normal aspect of our New Testament church services.

Just Do It!

We only had one time each week that our entire church family assembled together – our main Sunday morning worship service, the primary service frequented by most of those who visited our church for the first time. But, this also, was the only time where all 200 members of our congregation would be able to consistently pray together corporately.

Like the old Nike commercial says, "Just Do It!" As the senior pastor, I pioneered the entire plan, teaching, instruction, training of leaders, and the strategic-implementation of incorporating ten minutes of intercessory prayer into our main Sunday morning worship services. I never looked back and never regretted the day I made this critical decision.

In fact, making corporate-congregational prayer part of our main Sunday morning worship services was the single, most important (and best) decision that I made during my thirteen years of service as a senior pastor. If I ever pastor a church again, including corporate-congregational prayer as a normal-regular part of the main worship services will be the very first thing that I do.

Our Only Chance

As much as we all enjoy technology, the high-tech innovations of this generation can never replace the life changing presence and power of Jesus Christ, which only comes from the genuine ministry of the Holy Spirit, and is fueled by corporate-congregational intercessory prayer.

> *So he answered and said to me: "This is the word of the Lord to Zerubbabel: 'Not by might nor by power, but by My Spirit,' Says the Lord of hosts.*
>
> Zechariah 4:6

Humility, repentance, and a return to The Book of Acts model of including corporate-congregational prayer in our main worship services offer the only viable hope for genuine revival, and for the survival of America and the American church.

Chapter Eleven
A Word of Exhortation for Church Members

Please do not use this book as a tool to correct your pastor, dishonor his leadership, or to sow discord in the body of Christ by insinuating that he is hindering the flow of the Holy Spirit in your local church assembly if he doesn't dance to your tune and immediately include corporate prayer into your main Sunday church service.

Your Pastor is a Gift from Jesus

If you are a member of a local church family or serve on a church board, God has not ordained you to bring correction, instruction, guidance, or a word from the Lord to your pastor. Your pastor is the leader, not you! He has been placed in your local assembly, by Jesus, to bring correction, instruction, reproof, guidance, and a word from the Lord to you, not vice versa!

> *And He Himself [Jesus] gave some to be apostles, some prophets, some evangelists, and some pastors and teachers,*
>
> Ephesians 4:11

A pastor is a specific gift given to a local church congregation by Jesus Christ for the purpose of leading and feeding the church family (1 Peter 5:1-4).

Elders, deacons, and those who sit on church boards are there to lift up the hands of the pastor, to assist as needed, and to serve in a supportive role, but never in a leadership-directional capacity (Acts 6:1-4).

Jesus Christ is honored as you honor and respect the gift that He specifically gave to your local church – your pastor!

How to Appropriately Use this Book

Primarily, read this book for your own spiritual growth and enrichment. If you want to bless your pastor with this book without the attachment of any additional strings or expectations on your part, then that's fine, but leave it at that!

Your pastor is responsible to God for everyone in the church family, not just you! You may be on fire, excited, and ready for full-blown intercessory prayer to be an inclusive part of the main worship service in your church next Sunday. But there are probably some who are not ready for this, and your pastor has to guide the flock based on what everyone is able to handle without being broken.

So don't just automatically assume that your pastor is against having a time, or times of corporate prayer in your main worship service just because he is not moving as quickly as you may desire.

A Word of Exhortation for Church Members

Honor your pastor, make yourself available to help and serve, respect his decisions, and let him lead and guide the church. Remember, Jesus appointed your pastor to lead – not you!

Chapter Twelve
Developing a Culture of Corporate Prayer (for Pastors and Leaders)

I am, primarily, writing this chapter as a general guide to help senior pastors walk through the planning and development process of including corporate-congregational prayer into the structure of a main church service. Please remember, this is only a guide, and is not meant to serve as a detailed plan.

Although I will be specifically addressing pastors, and other church leaders, the contents we be helpful for all.

1. Only One Reason

There is only one reason that you should be thinking about including corporate-congregational prayer into the cultural structure of your main worship services. This is because corporate prayer pleases Jesus and is something which Jesus says He desires. "...It is written, My house shall be called a house of prayer" (Matthew 21:13).

2. You Must Be Committed

Corporate-congregational prayer in your main services cannot be a methodology or a drawing card that you just try. You must be completely convinced that this is the path Jesus wants you to follow, and your allegiance to Christ must be absolute, because your commitment will be tested!

3. Evaluate the Conditions of Your Flock

> *Be diligent to know the condition of your flocks, And pay attention to your herds;*
>
> Proverbs 27:23

What are the varied levels of growth, maturity, and spiritual comprehension of the believers that you shepherd? What kinds of prayer are they initially able to handle? Full-blown Book-of-Acts intercession with bold prayer in other tongues accompanied by groanings in the spirit? Or, would praying the written, promises of God from the Bible, in English, be a better starting point?

Are your congregants able to handle 10 to 15 minutes of corporate prayer? Or, would it be better to begin with 1 to 2 minutes?

You see, as the senior pastor in charge, you are accountable to Jesus for feeding and leading, the flock that you shepherd, into the place of corporate prayer. But, you must know the conditions of your flock in order to lead them with wisdom so they grow, mature, bear fruit, and are not broken in the process. Prayerfully evaluate your flock. Move slowly, methodically, and use wisdom.

4. Get Your Plan from God
I believe that using someone else's model is a mistake. I would even advise against using the plan which I undertook.

Every congregation resides in its own, unique-cultural setting. There are no hard, fast, applications and methodologies that can be applied across the board, other than to pray and to make sure that your prayers agree with the Holy Scriptures.

Get in your Bible. Study the Scriptures dealing with corporate prayer. Get alone with God, talk to Him, and find out the specific plan and structure of implementation that Jesus tells you will best fit your, specific church family. Write the plan down, share it, prepare, teach, develop leaders, implement it, and constantly evaluate everything that you are doing.

5. Write It Down for All to Read
Then the Lord answered me and said: "Write the vision And make it plain on tablets, That he may run who reads it."

Habakkuk 2:2

The number one mistake made by pastors, business people, and entrepreneurs is this: Failing to write down the plan, or the vision in a short, concise, easy-to-read manner so the staff, helpers, and congregation have something to unite to with their faith, their finances, and their service.

God did not just give us His plan for salvation – He wrote it down! Writing down a vision for corporate prayer (or for any plan) is a tool that connects the hearts of people to that vision so everyone is on the same page, knows what to do, and moves in the same direction.

The most successful pastors (and I have been with quite a few) have a written, vision and plan for every department and facet of the church's in-house and outreach ministries.

Do you want everything you do to be a success? Then, don't just wing it and fly by the seat of your pants! Learn to write everything down!

6. Prepare, Share, and Set a Target Date

I would advise against immediately changing the current structure of your main service. People need time to process any type of change. And yes, people will ask questions like, "Why do we all need to pray together? Why can't we just pray alone at home?"

Questions, of this nature and similar inquiries, do not indicate a lack of cooperation. They indicate a hesitancy of the individual to step out of their comfort zone into a new arena that will tremendously enrich their life. Your job, as the pastor, is to help each believer feel safe, and secure through the transition process. Solid-foundational instruction coupled with reassurance are invaluable.

Prepare to include corporate-congregational prayer into your main worship service by sharing the vision for corporate prayer with the church family 3-4 months in advance of the actual start up day.

Provide each church member with a written, copy of the vision. Set a target date and share something about corporate prayer every week leading up to the date of implementation.

7. Instructional Development

Spend ample time teaching your staff, other leaders, and the entire church family about, both, individual and corporate-congregational prayer. Share examples from the Book of Acts, and highlight the benefits, blessings, and miracles that occurred when the entire, early church family prayed together corporately in their main worship services.

8. How Should Prayer Be Structured?

Are you, as the senior pastor, initially going to lead the time of corporate-congregational prayer? Or, will you have a staff person or a trained church member lead?

Will topics, needs, or Scriptures be projected on a big screen? If someone other than you as the pastor leads prayer, what will be the written, parameters and guidelines for the leader to follow?

Again, there are no absolute ways to implement corporate prayer, but I would certainly have some prayer-specific parameters and guidelines. And, be sure to write them down!

If you decide to train a staff person or church member to lead prayer, make sure they are provided a written, job description complete with guidelines and parameters of functional-operating standards.

For instance, a staff person or church member leading prayer is functioning as a guide, and an on-site monitor, to keep prayer moving in a fluid direction. The prayer leader is not there to teach, preach, prophesy, give a word of knowledge, flow in other spiritual gifts, share what they are feeling in the spirit, or talk about a dream they had the previous evening.

No, the leader is there to implement the, written directives for corporate prayer, and nothing more. Incidentally, I would highly advise implementing similar guidelines for worship leaders.

Those who lead worship, likewise, are not in front of the congregation to put on a show, demonstrate their own-perceived spirituality, share a dream, give a prophecy, or determine the Holy Spirit's direction for the service. They humbly serve as a minstrel to lead praise and worship – nothing additional. The direction of a church service is always, and solely, overseen by the senior pastor!

Also, I would strongly advise against allowing anyone to supervise corporate prayer as the Spirit leads them, unless they are a servant-leader with years of proven experience, have a good report, and have demonstrated impeccable character and loyalty during tenuous, ministry times.

9. Developing Leaders
Anyone can be trained, but a loyal-faithful leader must be developed, and this is a process which requires time and investment!

Developing a Culture of Corporate Prayer

Always provide a leader in development with a clear, concise, written job description, complete with limitations and expectations.

Procedure to Train Prayer Leader:

- Provide adequate instruction and tools
- Have them watch you lead prayer
- Have them lead prayer with you
- Observe them leading prayer
- Evaluate (do after each step)
- Repeat any stage(s) needing more work
- Evaluate again
- Release individual to lead prayer by themselves

10. Implementation of Corporate Prayer

Follow the guidelines, procedures, and instructions you have given to your staff, leaders, helpers, and the congregation.

Don't overdo it! It is much wiser to begin with 1 to 2 minutes of corporate-congregational prayer in your main worship services, so that people leave wanting to pray more. Praying too long, initially, can actually wear people out and leave them feeling drained. Force yourself to move slowly and your church family will gradually mature into a mighty army of those who *know how to pray heaven into this earth!*

11. Evaluate in Your Weekly Staff Meetings

If you currently do not have weekly staff meetings then I would highly advise you to begin having them immediately.

If you, as the pastor are the only paid staff person, then hand-pick a few of those who help and serve, and meet with them weekly. Avoid meeting with just women. Make sure that you meet with at least the same number of men (preferably a few more) as women.

Our churches are being feminized due to a lack of strong-male leaders and role models. This why it is crucial for you to choose more men to meet with than women.

During your staff meetings, evaluate everything! Ask and discuss the following types of questions, and get feedback from everyone!

Did everything flow properly? Did everyone show up? Was everyone on time? Did everyone do their job and follow protocol? Were there any problems or surprises? Are we using the correct procedures? Is additional training or instruction needed? Should we restructure anything? Can we do anything better? Is the church family linking to the vision? Developing? Growing? Maturing?

Doing these types of staff meetings weekly keeps everyone, and every aspect of a local churches in-house and outreach ministries sharp, and imparts a spirit of excellence to the entire church family.

Presenting Another Book by Rev. Kim Wetteland

Buy it now at

www.ingramcontent.com/pod-product-compliance
Lightning Source LLC
LaVergne TN
LVHW051708080426
835511LV00017B/2789